D1404766

BACKYARD WILDLIFE

Centipedes

By Margo Gates

BLASTOFF! READERS

BELLWETHER MEDIA • MINNEAPOLIS, MN

Note to Librarians, Teachers, and Parents:

Blastoff! Readers are carefully developed by literacy experts and combine standards-based content with developmentally appropriate text.

Level 1 provides the most support through repetition of high-frequency words, light text, predictable sentence patterns, and strong visual support.

Level 2 offers early readers a bit more challenge through varied simple sentences, increased text load, and less repetition of high-frequency words.

Level 3 advances early-fluent readers toward fluency through increased text and concept load, less reliance on visuals, longer sentences, and more literary language.

Level 4 builds reading stamina by providing more text per page, increased use of punctuation, greater variation in sentence patterns, and increasingly challenging vocabulary.

Level 5 encourages children to move from "learning to read" to "reading to learn" by providing even more text, varied writing styles, and less familiar topics.

Whichever book is right for your reader, Blastoff! Readers are the perfect books to build confidence and encourage a love of reading that will last a lifetime!

This edition first published in 2014 by Bellwether Media, Inc.

No part of this publication may be reproduced in whole or in part without written permission of the publisher. For information regarding permission, write to Bellwether Media, Inc., Attention: Permissions Department, 5357 Penn Avenue South, Minneapolis, MN 55419.

Library of Congress Cataloging-in-Publication Data

Gates, Margo.
 Centipedes / by Margo Gates.
     pages cm. – (Blastoff! readers. Backyard wildlife)
 Audience: Grades K to 3.
 Includes bibliographical references and index.
 Summary: "Developed by literacy experts for students in kindergarten through grade three, this book introduces centipedes to young readers through leveled text and related photos"– Provided by publisher.
 ISBN 978-1-60014-918-4 (hardcover : alk. paper)
 1. Centipedes–Juvenile literature. I. Title.
 QL449.5.G38 2014
 595.6'2–dc23

2013000902

Printed in the United States of America, North Mankato, MN.

Contents

Centipedes are **arthropods**. They have long, flat bodies and many legs.

A centipede's body has many **segments**. Each segment has one pair of legs.

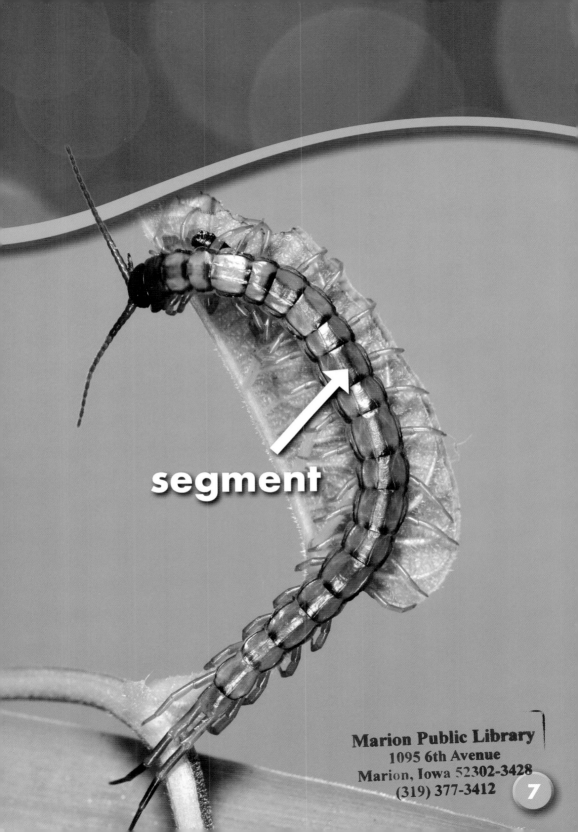

segment

7

Centipedes live
in dark places.
They make homes
under rocks,
leaves, and logs.

Female centipedes lay eggs. Some curl around their eggs to keep them safe.

Babies break
out of the eggs.
They **shed** their
exoskeletons
as they grow.

exoskeleton

Centipedes hunt at night. They eat **insects**, spiders, and other **prey**.

A centipede has front claws that are like **fangs**. **Venom** flows through them.

claws

Birds, frogs, and other **predators** eat centipedes.

Some large
centipedes eat
these predators.
This centipede
has a mouse!

Glossary

arthropods—animals with hard outer bodies and no backbones; arthropod bodies have segments.

exoskeletons—the hard outer coverings on the bodies of arthropods

fangs—long, sharp teeth; a centipede's front claws work like fangs.

insects—small animals with six legs and hard outer bodies; insect bodies are divided into three parts.

predators—animals that hunt other animals for food

prey—animals that are hunted by other animals for food

segments—parts that connect

shed—to drop or let fall off

venom—liquid that can kill an animal or make it unable to move

To Learn More

AT THE LIBRARY

Bodden, Valerie. *Centipedes.* Mankato, Minn.: Creative Education, 2011.

Ross, Tony. *Centipede's 100 Shoes.* New York, N.Y.: Holt, 2003.

Smithyman, Kathryn. *What Is an Arthropod?* New York, N.Y.: Crabtree Pub. Co., 2003.

ON THE WEB

Learning more about centipedes is as easy as 1, 2, 3.

1. Go to www.factsurfer.com.

2. Enter "centipedes" into the search box.

3. Click the "Surf" button and you will see a list of related Web sites.

With factsurfer.com, finding more information is just a click away.

Index

The images in this book are reproduced through the courtesy of: Pan Xubin, front cover; Attem, p. 5; Juan Martinez, pp. 7, 9 (middle), 17; Pietro Scozzari/ Age Fotostock, p. 9; Kevin Eng, p. 9 (left); W Deon, p. 9 (right); Michael D. Kern/ Nature Picture Library, p. 11; Animals Animals/ SuperStock, p. 13; Jose B. Ruiz/ Nature Picture Library, p. 15; Rechitan Sorin, p. 15 (left); Andrew Kerr, p. 15 (middle); FocusDzign, p. 15 (right); Boonchuay Promjiam, p. 19; Mircea Bezergheanu, p. 19 (left); Dennis Donohue, p. 19 (right); Tom McHugh/ Getty Images, p. 21.